THE
DUFFER'S
GUIDE TO
SKIING

John Fairbanks

Illustrations by Kim Leachman

COLUMBUS BOOKS

LONDON

Other books in the Duffer's series:

The Official Duffer's Rules of Golf (John Noble)
The Official Duffer's Rules of Tennis (Bob Adams)
The Duffer's Guide to Golf: A Second Slice (Gren)
The Duffer's Guide to Rugby (Gren)
The Duffer's Guide to Greece (Gren)
The Duffer's Guide to Spain (Gren)
The Duffer's Guide to Coarse Fishing (Mike Gordon)
The Duffer's Guide to Cricket (Gren)
The Duffer's Guide to Booze (Gren)
The Duffer's Guide to Rugby: Yet Another Try (Gren)
The Duffer's Guide to Snooker (Mike Gordon)
The Duffer's Guide to D-I-Y (Mike Gordon)
The Duffer's Guide to Getting Married (Gren)
The Duffer's Guide to Football (Gren)

First published in Great Britain in 1986 by
Columbus Books Limited
19-23 Ludgate Hill, London EC4M 7PD
Reprinted 1987

Printed by Redwood Burn Limited, Trowbridge, Wiltshire

Typeset by Cylinder Typesetting Limited,
85A Marchmont Street, London WC1N 1AL

ISBN 0 86287 291 X

WARNING

Skiing can damage your health

CONTENTS

Introduction

If you have bought this book in the hope of improving your skiing ability, we regret to inform you that you have wasted your money. But if you are one of the thousands of eager, unskilled duffers who live dangerously on the ski slopes each winter, or if you want to become one of them, read on. This book is definitely for you.

MOSTOVUM BRAKUM

Skiing is basically a simple sport and therefore an ideal pastime for the average duffer.

Indeed, the duffer connection is proven historical fact. Recently, in Sweden, a pair of 5,000-year-old skis were recovered from the depths of a bog. Who else but a duffer could lose his skis in a bog?

Skiing duffers are keen but incompetent, possess an acute sense of self-preservation and have a healthy disregard for the rules of the game. They search for success on skis in the same optimistic way that King Arthur's knights once sought the Holy Grail . . . and with even less chance of finding it.

Skiers must have stamina. Their typical day consists of four hours of exhausting instruction, a schnapps-sodden post mortem into the day's activities, and the nightly orgy known as après-ski. The day ends at 3 a.m., when sleep overcomes all carnal or alcoholic desires. That's why skiers must be tough.

Understanding the Holiday Brochure

Duffers are trusting souls who believe implicitly everything they are told. In order to help them separate truth from fiction we present a short guide to interpreting the language of the holiday brochure.

Alpine setting
– On a mountain peak
  miles from anywhere

Olde-worlde charm
– Decrepit

Recently built
– There's no roof yet

**Relaxed
atmosphere**
– Deserted

Table d'hôte
– Take it or leave it

10

In easy reach of all amenities
– Next door to railway/bus station

Home cooking
– Sauerkraut and chips

Services of resident representative
…if you can find him/her

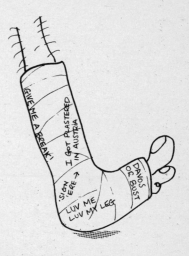

Fun-filled evenings
– Bingo in the dining room

Skiing fun
– Autographing plaster casts

11

Leading hotel in the area
- *Only* hotel in the area

Single room
- A room so small that when standing in the middle you can touch all four walls without moving

Double room
- As above but containing double bed

High season
– Resort overcrowded
 and expensive

Low season
– You'll be completely
 alone there, but it will
 still be expensive

Late season
– Overcrowded,
 exhorbitant,
 no snow

North-facing resort
– Daily blizzards
 and no sun – ever

Where to Go
and How to Get There

In the British Isles the annual ration of instant slush (laughingly referred to as 'snow') usually falls on Good Friday. It disappears overnight leaving behind utter chaos and giving the duffer no time to get his skis out of the coalshed.

So it you *really* want to ski you will have to travel abroad.

14

1. Car

Some duffers harbour romantic dreams of driving to the Alps, or whatever mountain range appeals to them. But after covering a thousand kilometres on the wrong side of icy roads, with the resident back-seat driver in full flow every inch of the way, the romance soon fades.

2. Coach

Coach travel is popular and cheap. Those who travel by this means are instantly recognizable. They are the people with swollen ankles and flat knee-caps.

3. Train

Many veterans 'get there' (in more ways than one) by train. The long journey is used as a mobile rehearsal for the après-ski orgies. Rail travel ensures that skiers arrive at their resort either drunk, in love, or both. On reflection, this is not a bad way to start any holiday.

4. Aeroplane

Duffers who fly to their holiday spot are also instantly identifiable. They do their skiing in lounge suits or lightweight dresses because their luggage, clearly marked 'Munich', has ended up in New Delhi.

People You Will Meet

During your visit to the ski slopes you will come into contact with several important people who are there solely to look after your welfare. However, as a duffer you should be aware that such care is going to cost you money.

1. The courier

The courier is all-powerful. His control of all the local rackets is absolute – so much so that he is known as 'The Godfather'. His 'family' acknowledges his right to command because he supplies something they all desperately need – skiers with money to burn.

2. The chambermaid

The chambermaid is female, probably of Yugoslavian extraction, and built like a Russian shot-putter. She speaks no English and is given to entering bedrooms at indelicate or inopportune moments. This ancient custom tends to result in her receiving generous tips from errant duffers in grateful recognition of her greatest asset – silence.

3. The ski instructor

There are two kinds of ski instructor . . . and duffers always get the bad ones. These blonde gods of the slopes are more interested in seduction than instruction. What they try to teach the more nubile members of their class gives a whole new meaning to the term 'ski jumping'.

4. The waitress

Because women increase in desirability relative to the amount of alcohol consumed by men waitresses are under constant attack by drunken skiers. However these embattled females safeguard their virtue by saying 'no' (in eight languages) and protect their bottoms from pinching fingers by wearing reinforced nylon knickers.

Skiers' Gear

Duffers can increase their chances of survival on the slopes by dressing the part and having the right sports equipment. Wearing the correct dress will also give the completely false impression that the duffer can ski. For those who wish to gain acceptance into skiing circles, or to impress gullible members of the opposite sex, the right gear is essential.

But just what is the correct attire for skiing? Consult the following pages and you'll get the general idea.

1. Trousers

Duffers spend a great deal of their time on the piste with their backsides planted firmly in the snow. This often leads to a medical condition known as 'polar bear's bum'. One way to avoid icicles forming round the private parts is to avoid skiing altogether. Alternatively, buy a pair of well-padded waterproof ski pants.

2. Anorak

Duffers are generally broke. But no expense should be spared when kitting out for an alpine expedition. Groundsheets are no substitute for custom-built anoraks. A sudden gust of wind beneath your 'poncho' could result in an unexpected session of hang-gliding on skis.

3. Gloves

It is distressing to see skiers carried off to hospital with their schnapps flask frozen to their fingers. The risk of amputation (and subsequent damage to the schnapps flask) may be avoided by the wearing of suitable gloves.

4. Hats

Skiing duffers have a habit of vanishing at high
speed into the depths of snow drifts. To avoid
ensuing oblivion, it is wise to choose highly
coloured headgear. Many an entombed skier
has been saved because his technicolor hat was
visible from the air.

5. Sun glasses

Rotten skiers can never have a large enough supply of excuses, which they use to explain away the scars of battle or their reluctance to risk acquiring such. A suitable pair of 'shades' give you the ideal reason for not appearing on the piste, because you can wander around complaining of snow blindness.

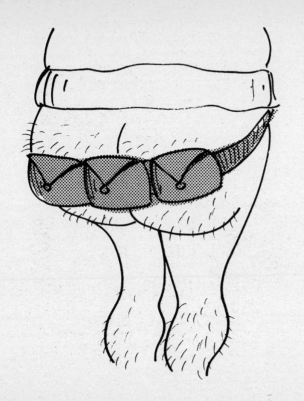

6. Belt

A 'banana belt', so called because of its shape, is used to carry vital survival gear such as cigarettes, matches and medicinal schnapps. Because of the way it is worn duffers refer to it as a 'bum belt'.

29

7. Bindings

Skiers remain attached to their skis by virtue of the bindings. It is the failure of this fitting to release the foot when the skier falls over that causes so many fractured legs. This is why skiers are so devout. One of the most commonly heard prayers on the ski slopes is 'Oh God! I hope the bindings work!'

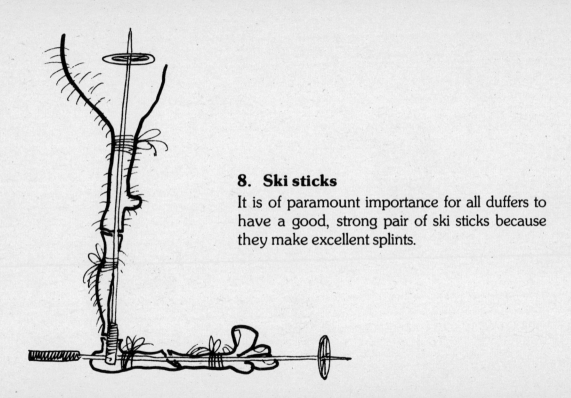

8. Ski sticks

It is of paramount importance for all duffers to have a good, strong pair of ski sticks because they make excellent splints.

9. Skis

Duffers should not try to take their own skis abroad. In the hands of a semi-inebriated duffer a pair of carelessly carried skis becomes a lethal weapon.

10. Boots

Ski boots make good doorstops, excellent cat-scarers and on occasion very deep ashtrays. They even come in handy for skiing. But the heavy plastic, high-ankled, one-piece monstrosities are definitely not made for walking.

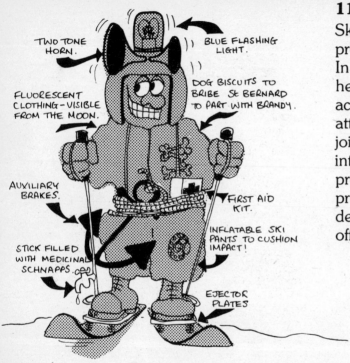

TWO TONE HORN.

BLUE FLASHING LIGHT.

FLUORESCENT CLOTHING – VISIBLE FROM THE MOON.

DOG BISCUITS TO BRIBE St BERNARD TO PART WITH BRANDY.

AUXILIARY BRAKES.

FIRST AID KIT.

INFLATABLE SKI PANTS TO CUSHION IMPACT!

STICK FILLED WITH MEDICINAL SCHNAPPS.

EJECTOR PLATES.

11. Duffer's survival outfit

Skiing is a dangerous sport as duffers are accident-prone virtually by definition.

In view of this unholy combination a comprehensive insurance policy should always be acquired prior to any other item of equipment or attire. Now that you are well on the way to joining the ranks of the ski-slope kamikazes, intent on defying all the laws of nature and self-preservation, you would be well advised to provide yourself in addition with this specially designed duffer's survival outfit, unselfishly offered by the author to whomsoever is interested.

Skiing Types

The members of any group of skiers have at least one thing in common: like lemmings, they have all set out to do themselves harm. Other than that, in any such group certain distinctive types are likely to emerge. They each have a specific function and are easy to recognize. Even duffers will soon know who they are.

1. The group leader

Duffers need someone who will round everyone up, keep an eye on the luggage, marshal and entertain the kids, check on departure times, and generally take care of things. If they can't find such a person before the trip starts they don't worry. They know that within minutes of the group assembling the unofficial leader will take command. He always does.

2. Beautiful women

Any man who takes a good-looking woman on a skiing holiday, or who successfully chats one up on the journey to his holiday venue, is wasting both his time and his money. This is because all the beautiful women are reserved exclusively for the ski instructors and will be claimed by them within minutes of arrival.

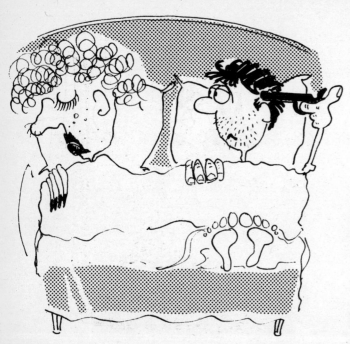

3. Wallflowers

In the interests of sexual harmony each group should include only ladies of indeterminate age and plain appearance. As the alcohol consumption rises, these women will attract more and more male attention. It is not for nothing that the male skiers' anthem is a song containing the immortal lines: 'I've never been to bed with an ugly woman, but I've sure woken up with a few.'

4. The siren

In any group of skiers there is always a *femme fatale*. Beautifully groomed, she wears expensive skintight clothes and is drenched in exotic perfume. Although she never skis her trademark is her fashionable après-ski footwear, which resembles a pair of dead Shetland ponies.

5. Male skiers

It doesn't matter whether the male members of the group are handsome, plain or downright ugly. No one will care. The only assets a man needs are a strong head, a well-filled wallet and complete immunity to brewer's droop.

6. The minders

Present in every group of skiers are several men trained to defend their friends from the vile attentions of foreigners. These heroes can be identified by their green-striped rugby shirts, an insatiable thirst for beer, an inexhaustible repertoire of obscene songs and a very narrow space between the top of their heads and their eyebrows.

7. The expert

The expert may be found strolling about the resort telling impressive tales about his skiing exploits. He is always dressed in the best ski clothing and carries the finest equipment money can buy. He knows all the instructors by name and is constantly seen in the smartest cafés surrounded by a group of devotees. But strangely enough he is never actually seen skiing.

8. The retired Indian Army Colonel

This man is easily recognized owing to his florid complexion and unquenchable thirst for pink gins. He never skis but is a priceless asset to any group because of his unrivalled expertise in quelling rebellious natives.

43

9. The ex-matron type

For administrative reasons this woman is welcome in any group. She has absolutely no interest in skiing but knows exactly how to bend intractable hoteliers and bureaucrats to her awesome will. She always has a small watch pinned to her intimidating bosom and is paranoid about the lack of hygiene in foreign countries.

10. The interpreter

The resident group interpreter is never fluent in any foreign language but is capable of uttering important phrases, such as 'Does this wine contain glycol?' Because of his position he learns many secrets concerning the financial and sexual affairs of the group. For this reason the average interpreter never wants for anything.

11. The lecher

Dracula, the resident sex fiend, is seldom seen before sunset. Remarkable for his sallow complexion, bloodshot eyes and habit of blinking rapidly if accidentally exposed to daylight, he will chase anything in skirts except Gordon Highlanders and members of the Greek National Guard.

46

First Steps

The trouble with skiing is that it looks easy. But when you stand on skis for the first time the initial reaction is one of panic. This is hardly surprising. After all, your feet have suddenly become three feet longer at either end and have acquired a mind of their own.

After many lessons you will be able to stand unaided, turn round and even walk again. You will then attempt to copy the experts zooming about in the snow around you. When you do finally get moving you will make the most traumatic discovery of your life.

There are no brakes.

How to Stop

It is claimed that yodelling is done by singing and shivering at the same time. A similar noise is made by duffers as they desperately try to bring their uncontrolled downhill run to a painless halt. They usually succeed by using one of the four unofficial methods listed here, but they seldom manage to do it painlessly.

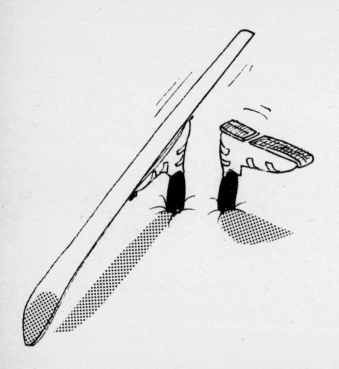

1. The nose dive

A nose dive always begins as an attempt to perform a 'snowplough'. Although this manoeuvre causes the legs to slow down it does not stop the shoulders from advancing. So the trunk bends remorselessly forward until the nose bites deep into the snow. This is an efficient but eye-watering way to stop.

2. The sideways collapse

When a skier is moving at a fairly slow pace all that is needed to halt his momentum is to allow a leg to buckle. The sudden transferring of all his weight will cause the skier to fall. It is best to collapse downhill because the increased impact results in a deeper 'bite' into the snow. This produces extremely effective brake-power.

3. The 'grab-it'

After reaching a high speed, the desperate skier's only hope is to grab hold of a stationary object as he hurtles past. Unfortunately it is not always possible to retain such a hold. The net result may be a change of direction at a much greater velocity.

4. The only alternative

When maximum speed has been attained and all other methods have failed, the only alternative left to the doomed skier is to hit something solid. This is the most effective, dramatic and unfailingly painful way of stopping.

Technical Expressions

Duffers should carefully read and memorize the following information. By doing so they will at least be able to talk skiers' language.

Chair lift

A series of seats, open to the elements and fixed to a continuous belt, used to convey skiers to the slopes. It is a cold way to travel, and should the lift break down skiers may contract a form of frostbite, peculiar to chair-lift users, called 'iced anus'.

Cable car
A covered-in version of the chair-lift, not to be mistaken for a vehicle used by the Post Office to deliver telegrams.

Schuss

Rarely used for calming fractious Tyrolean children, this onomatopoeic term describes a straight downhill run.

Stem turn

Nothing to do with flower-arranging: just a method of stopping or changing direction.

Drag lift

An apparatus that literally drags skiers up a slope – not solely a means of carrying men who have a peculiar dress sense and a strange outlook on life.

Piste

This is the skiing area. To go on the piste means to go skiing, not to embark on a pub crawl.

Slalom

A type of race – not a Hebrew greeting.

Wedeln

A swinging action performed at high speed. Duffers find this difficult to do and even harder to say.

Traverse

To move diagonally across a slope. The amount of alcohol normally consumed by the duffer means that sideways is his normal direction of travel.

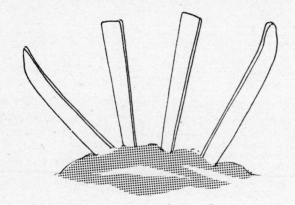

Snowplough

Strangely enough, this is a method of stopping that requires strong legs and the adoption of an embarrassing posture.

Blue – black – red

Ski runs are classified using colour codes: blue for 'beginners', red for 'intermediate', black for 'advanced' skiers. As far as the duffer is concerned, the correct definitions are blue for bruising, red for blood and black for funeral.

Cheers!

When they are not skiing, receiving first aid or making love, skiers drink. Indeed, there is little else they can do in their spare time. Any duffer contemplating a skiing holiday who cannot already drink a Liverpool docker under the table should contemplate a serious course of training.

1. Glühwein

Mulled red wine, or glühwein, is popular with skiers. It has a bigger punch than Barry McGuigan and is often used as an opiate by those who have rashly agreed to undertake a hair-raising moonlight toboggan ride.

2. White wine

Because of its spectacular 'morning-after' qualities white wine (with or without glycol) is known respectfully as 'white lightning' in the skiing fraternity.

BEFORE

AFTER

3. Schnapps

Schnapps is a most useful drink. It kills pain instantly, provides both warmth and courage and is therefore of great practical value to skiers. It has one further use which endears it to duffers in particular: when administered to young ladies it makes the pure willing to be soiled and turns those of doubtful virtue into dead certs.

4. Beer

Most continentals are weaned on alcohol and tend to cut their teeth on litre beer mugs. Duffers are warned never to enter into competition with such people, most of whom are incipient alcoholics even before they leave school. Many a stalwart of his local hostelries has sunk without trace during an alpine boat race.

Skiers' Fare

Duffers seldom eat breakfast. In hotel dining rooms the early-morning cathedral calm is broken only by the occasional low moan, or the sound of antacids fizzing.

However, later in the day there will come a time when even the duffer decides that lining his stomach in preparation for the evening's liquid onslaught would be quite a good idea.

1. Goulash soup

The traditional skiers' lunch is a bowl of hot, spicy goulash soup, after which some people are afflicted by a condition known to the medical profession as 'Hitler's Revenge'. The symptoms of this distressing ailment are a desire to take up permanent residence in the nearest toilet and a determination to stick to chips in future.

2. Sauerkraut

Sadistic foreign cooks delight in offering sauer-kraut to unsuspecting skiers. Described as sour pickled cabbage, it has a distinctive aroma of rotting footwear. Such is the effect of its offensive pong that only pickled duffers can eat it with impunity.

68

3. Speck

The piquancy of sauerkraut pales into insignificance when compared to the smell of *speck*. This alleged bacon dish has an awesome stench capable of buckling bomb-proof doors. The claim that it is bacon has never been tested.

69

Après-ski

Après-ski is a nightly series of orgiastic events noted for its air of frenzied licentiousness. Duffers claim that had the Emperor Nero known about après-ski he would have patented it.

1. The cultural exchange

This evening's entertainment begins as a performance of songs and dances of the region given by the villagers. It ends with some duffers trying to discover how national costumes are made by undressing the dancers whilst others teach the folk group a few traditional English airs such as 'Maggie May' and 'How I Love My Mother-in-law'.

71

2. The moonlight toboggan ride

Many duffers, often after an excess of glühwein, have hit on the idea of making a romantic moonlit trip down a mountain on a toboggan. However, very few reach the bottom on board their chosen conveyance. Most people simply fall off at the first bend, while others seem prone to repeated collisions which cause the sleds to disintegrate.

3. The fondue evening

A 'fondue' is a d-i-y meal cooked at the table by immersing skewered cubes of steak into bowls of hot oil heated by small meths-burners. Because such meals are inevitably accompanied by plentiful amounts of red wine, they can be lengthy, hilarious and sometimes dangerous affairs. It is not unknown for the table to be set on fire — which proves what most of us have always thought, that eating foreign food *is* a risky business.

4. The ski instructors' ball

This cultural highlight of the season is organized for a specific reason. It is designed to demonstrate that instructors are human beings and not just skiing machines. So successful are they that their annual ball is known to many as the Carnal Carnival.

Medical matters

Skiing is a tough sport. Accidents can and do occur with monotonous regularity. Duffers have broken their legs whilst walking down aircraft steps, crossing the street and even by falling out of bed. Occasionally the same thing happens while they're on the piste, too.

FOR VALOUR

1. Getting plastered

Sooner or later all skiers are awarded the Alpine VC – a plaster cast. These awards are much sought after because (a) they mean that the holders need no longer risk life and limb on the slopes and (b) gypsum is a powerful aphrodisiac. In case you should doubt the veracity of (b), just bear in mind that the overwhelming number of people who have lost their virginity whilst immobilized makes it incontrovertible fact.

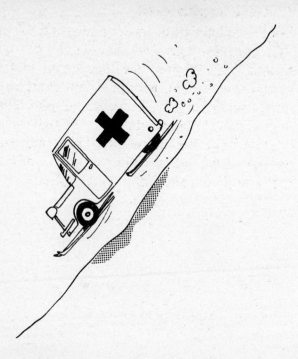

2. Mountain rescue

Most injured skiers are delivered to the doctor by means of the blood wagon. This stretcher on skis is guided down the mountain by a team of volunteer rescuers. Frequent pauses are made during the descent to administer medicinal schnapps, mainly to the rescuers. Eventually, against all odds, the patient reaches the doctor.

3. The doctor

The alpine doctor is an expert in the treatment of bone fractures and has an unrivalled understanding of insurance policies. Having spent years listening to the ravings of injured foreign skiers, he has a limited but spectacularly obscene vocabulary in various languages.

The surgeries of ski doctors are usually known as Colditz, because unless you are able to settle the bill on the spot you will find they are escape-proof.

4. The hospital

The main feature of most hospitals attached to ski resorts is that the wards are staffed by nuns. Therefore the sole method of treatment consists of liberal sprinklings of holy water twice a day.

Next Year?

Most skiers return home shattered in mind and body, in debt to various agencies, twitching from nervous exhaustion, threatened with divorce, and suffering the agonies of advanced alcoholism. But in spite of all this they are usually undeterred. As soon as they can manage their crutches they hobble round to the travel agency to book next year's holiday. They do so because all skiers are gluttons for punishment and eternal optimists.

Once a duffer, always a duffer...